THE MORNING MEDITATION JOURNAL

THE MORNING MEDITATION JOURNAL

Inspiring Prompts to Start Your Day with Clarity and Perspective

Worthy Stokes

ROCKRIDGE PRESS

For general information on our other products and services or to obtain technical support, please contact our Customer Care Department within the United States at (866) 744-2665, or outside the United States at (510) 253-0500.

Rockridge Press publishes its books in a variety of electronic and print formats. Some content that appears in print may not be available in electronic books, and vice versa.

TRADEMARKS: Rockridge Press and the Rockridge Press logo are trademarks or registered trademarks of Callisto Media Inc. and/or its affiliates, in the United States and other countries, and may not be used without written permission. All other trademarks are the property of their respective owners. Rockridge Press is not associated with any product or vendor mentioned in this book.

Series Designer: Lisa Forde
Interior and Cover Designer: John Clifford
Art Producer: Hannah Dickerson
Editor: John Makowski
Production Editor: Matthew Burnett
Production Manager: Jose Olivera

Author photo courtesy of David Genik Photography

ISBN: Print 978-1-648-76985-6
R0

THIS JOURNAL BELONGS TO

STEVEN SMITH

*"When you arise in the morning, think of what
a precious privilege it is to be alive—to breathe,
to think, to enjoy, to love."*

MARCUS AURELIUS

INTRODUCTION

Welcome to *The Morning Meditation Journal*—your daily guide to inspiration, clarity, and writing as a path of presence. Maybe you picked up this journal because you're feeling stressed and anxious, or maybe you have been struggling privately with depression. Perhaps you want to deepen your relationship with yourself, expand your perspective, access new awareness, and become more productive. Whether you hope to develop a completely new meditation practice or deepen a current one, these guided meditation exercises and corresponding writing prompts are designed to support you. Any time we make an effort to start our day with thoughtful intention, these morning moments of practiced awareness strengthen our resilience and prepare us for what's ahead. My hope is that this journal will inspire you to develop greater confidence, feel more joyful, feel less anxious, and more at ease with life.

My name is Worthy Stokes. As a polytrauma brain injury survivor who lives with multisensory loss, for years I have relied heavily on mindfulness as a personal resource, and I have been teaching meditation and coaching since 2018. In my personal meditation practice, which began in 2008, I have experimented with multiple techniques that range from one hour sits and recitations of mantras to weeks of solitary retreat. Collectively, the practices and prompts I have prepared for this journal reflect the most essential gems of wisdom I know. In fact, each meditation is thoughtfully designed to illuminate and nurture your magnificent potential at the nexus of science, soma, and soul. As you explore this contemplative landscape, my wish is that you will meet your deepest self, activate your innermost technology, and harness the power of your heart, mind, and breath to realize: *The miracle is you.*

The Power of Practicing Presence

Meditation is a way for you to experience greater amounts of joy and feel empowered to face challenges with thoughtful curiosity. Simply being still, turning inward, and beginning the day with intention is known to have a measurable positive impact. As you learn to connect with your inner wisdom and creativity, every morning can be transformed into an opportunity to strengthen feelings of gratitude, hope, courage, loving-kindness, and compassion—for yourself and for others.

How to Use This Journal

The Morning Meditation Journal is designed to be used in a way that feels comfortable and relaxed, while also inviting you to lean into the effort required to establish a regular morning meditation practice. You will see the most transformation if you choose to practice daily, at the same time every morning, but you may also choose to start more slowly and do it weekly or whenever you have 10 minutes to spare. However you choose to practice, these exercises are simple, effective, and easy to follow. Simply open the journal, find the day you would like to explore, and begin.

DAILY MEDITATION PRACTICES

Every day begins with a short, guided meditation exercise to help you connect with your inner landscape and ease into a mindful flow. These practices are designed to take approximately five minutes and will set you up for a positive day. As your awareness expands and evolves, you will notice more, worry less, and tune into joy with natural ease.

INSPIRATIONAL JOURNAL PROMPTS

After you've taken the time to mindfully check in, take as long as you like to respond to the writing prompts that accompany each meditation (I recommend at least five minutes). By meditating *and* journaling, you further integrate mindful awareness, bridge cognitive attention with somatic intuition, and enhance creative flow. These prompts encourage reflective thinking, which is meant to fasten your awareness to what you dream of, hope for, and intend.

SETTING INTENTIONS

By setting an intention for the day, you interact directly with the neuro-plasticity of your mind. The word "intention" is derived from the Latin *intendere* or *intentio*, which means both "stretching" and "purpose." By choosing to consciously attune to your "purpose" of the day, you invite your brain to "stretch" its attention, build new neural networks, and orient itself to joy. In setting your intention for the day, think about what kind of energy you want to bring to your day. How can your actions and choices align with what you value or to inspire others? How do you hope to show up in the world, for your community and for yourself?

I congratulate you for giving yourself the gift of this book and exploring these exercises, and I hope you find the peace, clarity, and inspiration you seek. May you be happy and at ease as you embrace the joyful, creative possibility that awaits you in the days ahead.

_____

_____

3. What feels different about breathing through your nose versus breathing through your mouth?

_____

_____

_____

_____

MY INTENTION(S) FOR TODAY:

_____

_____

_____

_____

_____

_____

DAY 3

HUM OF JOY

Stand with your feet hip-width apart and place your hands gently on your hips. Soften your gaze and rest your eyes on a point in your surroundings. Inhale slowly and begin to hum quietly on your out breath. Do this several times. As you feel the hum moving within you, imagine it carries the quality of joy. Take this quiet sound of joy into your day. Tune into it whenever you wish.

1. How does your thinking change when, consciously or unconsciously, joy is present?

_____

_____

_____

_____

2. Describe how one part of your body would benefit from joy traveling through or across it.

_____

_____

_____

_____

3. I will invite the vibrations of joy into my day when I am:

_____

_____

_____

_____

MY INTENTION(S) FOR TODAY:

_____

_____

_____

_____

_____

_____

DAY 4

OCEAN OF PEACE

Sit in a comfortable position and visualize gentle waves. Imagine one of them is rolling gently toward you. As if you are surrounded by an ocean of peace, notice the water's calm strength. Breathing with your mouth closed, let yourself be enveloped by a warm current. Bring your awareness back to the moment and notice any sensations. Remember this wave of peace whenever you wish.

1. When grounded in an experience of peace, how do you feel?

_____

_____

_____

_____

2. By bringing a wave of peace into my life each day, I can:

_____

_____

_____

_____

3. How would our world be different if everyone knew how to visualize peace?

_____

_____

_____

_____

MY INTENTION(S) FOR TODAY:

_____

_____

_____

_____

_____

_____

DAY 5

LET THERE BE SPACE FOR HOPE

Settle into a comfortable position. Soften any tension in your body. Without trying to control your breath, gently inhale and exhale naturally. Begin to imagine a space behind your mind's eye. As this space expands, give yourself permission to fill it with hope. Rest in this awareness and notice any color or shape that comes to mind. As often as possible throughout your day, let there be this space for hope.

1. What words or expressions do you associate with hope?

_____

_____

_____

_____

2. Think of a moment when you were filled with hope, when hope seemed to be bursting forth from you, and describe how it felt.

_____

_____

_____

_____

3. One person whom I can share my hope with is:

_____

_____

_____

_____

MY INTENTION(S) FOR TODAY:

_____

_____

_____

_____

_____

_____

DAY 6

LOVING-KINDNESS

Choose a comfortable position. Invite a sense of well-being into this moment. Sitting quietly, repeat the following for several moments: *May I be happy. May I be healthy. May I be at ease with this life*. Next, think of a friend or loved one you cherish. With this person in mind, repeat the practice: *May you be happy. May you be healthy. May you be at ease with this life.*

1. Reflect on your experience with this practice. What came up for you?

_____

_____

_____

_____

2. Research shows that practicing kindness toward yourself reduces stress levels in your body. How can you be more kind toward yourself today?

_____

_____

_____

_____

3. When you take time to extend kindness to yourself and others, how does it feel?

_____

_____

_____

_____

MY INTENTION(S) FOR TODAY:

_____

_____

_____

_____

_____

_____

DAY 7

ACTIVATE CREATIVITY

Begin by placing your hands over your heart and turning your attention inward. Offer a quiet prayer of gratitude for your ability to imagine new ideas. With your eyes softly closed, visualize your mind illuminated with light. Thank your mind for its strength to transform. Imagine a thread of light connecting your mind and your heart. Bring a new sense of creativity to every moment of your day.

1. Every moment is an opportunity to be creative. To what moments in your coming day can you add creativity?

_____

_____

_____

_____

2. Is there a difference between *allowing* yourself to be creative and *trying* to be creative?

_____

_____

_____

_____

3. An instance where I can bring physical creativity into my day is:

_____

_____

_____

_____

MY INTENTION(S) FOR TODAY:

_____

_____

_____

_____

_____

_____

DAY 8

YOUR RIVER OF INNER SILENCE

Find a comfortable, quiet place. Rest your hands wherever you wish, relax your fingers, and loosen your jaw. As you soften your gaze or close your eyes, tap into the silence resting within. Imagine a river of quietude starting deep at the center of your body and flowing out through all your limbs and the top of your head. As you feel this river of inner silence moving through you, tap into the flow of your breath. Notice when your day seems to be fluid with ease.

1. How is your relationship with silence? For example, does inner silence feel comforting?

_____

_____

_____

_____

2. Do you feel as though you are able to trust your inner wisdom? Why or why not?

_____

_____

_____

_____

3. What can you pay attention to in your life to discern whether you are _"in the flow"_?

_____

_____

_____

_____

MY INTENTION(S) FOR TODAY:

_____

_____

_____

_____

_____

_____

DAY 9

MINDFUL NOURISHMENT

Begin by softening your gaze or closing your eyes. Bring your awareness to your breath and settle into an easy, natural rhythm of breathing. Take this time to reflect on feeling nourished. With each breath, transform self-judgment about food into curiosity. With your mind's eye, imagine a day of mindful eating—being fully present in the act of nourishing your body. Resting one hand on your heart and the other on your belly, invite the fullness of peace.

1. Bringing your full attention to a recent meal and reflect on how present you were.

_____

_____

_____

_____

2. Think of a food you eat often and describe what you like most about it.

_____

_____

_____

_____

3. How is mindful eating different from distracted eating?

_____

_____

_____

_____

MY INTENTION(S) FOR TODAY:

_____

_____

_____

_____

_____

_____

DAY 10

BODY SCAN

This exercise is done lying down with your eyes closed. Breathing naturally, begin to scan your body for sensations. As you inhale, deliberately tense and hold your muscles. As you exhale, gently release the tension. Repeat this process and notice the parts of your body that begin to relax. Continue to mindfully breathe for several moments.

1. How do you feel different after completing a mindful body scan?

_____

_____

_____

_____

2. How can you take better care of your body?

_____

_____

_____

_____

3. What are two simple things you can do today to support your body's well-being?

_____

_____

_____

_____

MY INTENTION(S) FOR TODAY:

_____

_____

_____

_____

_____

_____

DAY 11

EMBRACE GRATITUDE

In a seated position, rest your hands wherever you wish. Breathe through your nose with your mouth closed and tune into your inner space. Turn your attention to something in your life you feel grateful for. Think on why you feel this appreciation. With every inhalation and exhalation, mentally say thank you. In moments of stress today, take time to recall one thing you feel gratitude for.

1. Who can you intentionally choose to share gratitude with today?

_____

_____

_____

_____

2. Describe the physical sensation or emotions you feel when you share gratitude with someone.

_____

_____

_____

_____

3. One thing I have not said thank you for in a long time is:

_____

_____

_____

_____

MY INTENTION(S) FOR TODAY:

_____

_____

_____

_____

_____

_____

DAY 12

SOUND MEDITATION

Choose a comfortable place to sit or lie on your back. As you rest your eyes, tune into the acoustic soundscape of your surroundings. Let sounds come and go with ease. If there are no sounds, rest in this moment of silence. As you experience the soundscape of the world in this moment, take some time to appreciate your ability to hear music, the sound of someone's voice, nature.

1. What music do you listen to most and why? How does music make you feel?

_____

_____

_____

_____

2. If you take time today to listen to sounds around you, what might be different for you?

_____

_____

_____

_____

3. Do you feel as though others take time to listen to you? Do you feel heard?

_____

_____

_____

_____

MY INTENTION(S) FOR TODAY:

_____

_____

_____

_____

_____

_____

DAY 13

MINDFUL COMMUNICATION

Rest quietly and connect with the present moment to consider your communication style. Reflect with clarity and curiosity, but without self-judgment. Bring an upcoming conversation to your mind's eye and imagine approaching it with mindful attention. If you feel anxious about expressing yourself, choose a mantra for inner support. Select a word to use as an anchor in moments of stress and repeat it silently: presence, harmony, compassion, courage, or curiosity.

1. Communicating from a place of confidence and curiosity is a gift to others. What and with whom will you communicate mindfully today?

_____

_____

_____

_____

2. Think about a moment of mindful communication, focusing on your body. How does your body feel in moments of mindful communication? How do you communicate nonverbally?

_____

_____

_____

_____

3. Describe a moment when you can bring compassion into your communication. What is it you do differently?

_____

_____

_____

_____

MY INTENTION(S) FOR TODAY:

_____

_____

_____

_____

_____

_____

DAY 14

PRACTICE RAIN

By using a framework known as RAIN, which was developed by Michele McDonald and adapted by psychologist and meditation teacher Tara Brach, you can set an intention to practice mindfulness at any time by following these four cues: *Recognize* what is happening around you, or inside of you. *Allow* the experience without judging it. *Investigate* the moment as it is, with interest and care. *Nurture* yourself by practicing self-compassion.

1. How can you practice RAIN throughout your day, in simple ways?

_____

_____

_____

_____

2. Reflect on how judgmental you are with yourself. Could RAIN support you to be less so?

_____

_____

_____

_____

3. Describe one time you gave yourself the gift of self-compassion.

_____

_____

_____

_____

MY INTENTION(S) FOR TODAY:

_____

_____

_____

_____

_____

_____

DAY 15

CONNECT WITH OPEN AWARENESS

Settle in for a gentle practice of nondirective attention, also known as open awareness. As you rest in the present moment, abide with what is, without trying to change it. Whenever you notice a thought, feeling, or physical sensation, let it arise. Open awareness is a practice of awakening to the subtle qualities of your attention. There is nothing to do or accomplish. In staying open and aware, you naturally become more present, more attentive, and more relaxed.

1. What are some positive thoughts that usually go unnoticed?

_____

_____

_____

_____

2. Describe the physical sensations that accompany practicing open awareness.

_____

_____

_____

_____

3. An experience I can bring open awareness into is:

_____

_____

_____

_____

MY INTENTION(S) FOR TODAY:

_____

_____

_____

_____

_____

_____

DAY 16

EMBODY SELF-COMPASSION

Place your hands over your heart and turn your attention inward. With your eyes softly closed, visualize your heart illuminated with light. Thank it for its strength to transform. As you inhale and exhale with ease, envision this inner light expanding. Notice the gentle presence of warm, heartfelt compassion. Return to the present moment and carry this sensation into your day.

1. What are some feelings, thoughts, and sensations this meditation brought up for you?

_____

_____

_____

_____

2. What does self-compassion mean to you?

_____

_____

_____

_____

3. How often do you show compassion toward yourself and others?

_____

_____

_____

_____

MY INTENTION(S) FOR TODAY:

_____

_____

_____

_____

_____

_____

DAY 17

LAUGHING MEDITATION

Begin by warming up with light clapping. Quietly start chanting *Ho, ho, ha, ha, ha*, exaggerating the *ha* on your exhale. Because your brain is unable to distinguish between real laughter and fake laughter, give yourself permission to chuckle until it feels real. As you clap, chant, and chuckle, notice whether you can laugh at the silliness.

1. When can you choose to laugh in moments where you normally stifle your laughter?

_____

_____

_____

_____

2. When did you last have a really good laugh?

_____

_____

_____

_____

3. Reflect on a moment when someone shared the medicine of laughter with you.

_____

_____

_____

_____

MY INTENTION(S) FOR TODAY:

_____

_____

_____

_____

_____

_____

DAY 18

INNER SMILE FOR EXPANDING JOY

Begin by closing your eyes and relaxing your whole body. Breathing naturally, connect with your inner landscape and loosen the muscles around your face, especially the jaw. With your eyes closed, think of something that brings you joy, and smile. After you experience the sensation of your outer smile, relax your mouth. This time, imagine yourself smiling again on the inside, without moving your face. Can you feel your inner smile?

1. A reason in my life for smiling is:

_____

_____

_____

_____

2. A person who often brings me joy is _____. Being with them uplifts me because:

_____

_____

_____

_____

3. How might practicing your inner smile today help you feel more at ease?

_____

_____

_____

_____

MY INTENTION(S) FOR TODAY:

_____

_____

_____

_____

_____

_____

DAY 19

POSITIVE ATTUNEMENT

Attunement means to come into harmony with something. The practice of positive attunement is the art of noticing a positive characteristic in someone you meet or acknowledging a pleasant element of your environment. Rest in a comfortable space and take a moment to look around. Notice one simple thing that you find inspiring, comforting, or beautiful. Throughout the day, practice attuning to what is positive.

1. Thinking about the day ahead, what is something positive you can attune to?

_____

_____

_____

_____

2. A positive memory that can be supportive of me today is:

_____

_____

_____

_____

3. Reflecting on today's practice, describe the role your physical body plays in positive attunement.

_____

_____

_____

_____

MY INTENTION(S) FOR TODAY:

_____

_____

_____

_____

_____

_____

DAY 20

MINDFUL BREATHING

When thoughts or feelings seem overwhelming, mindful breathing is a support you can always count on. Rest in a comfortable space and bring your attention to your breath. As you inhale and exhale naturally, invite your breath to be fluid. Instead of judging thoughts or feelings, let them rest inside of your breath. Experience the way mindful breathing can bring comfort and clarity. Mindful breathing is a simple way to come home to yourself whenever you need it.

1. What thoughts arise when you breathe mindfully?

_____

_____

_____

_____

2. When I experience anxiety or stress, I can take good care of myself by:

_____

_____

_____

_____

3. Today I can practice mindful breathing whenever I feel:

_____

_____

_____

_____

MY INTENTION(S) FOR TODAY:

_____

_____

_____

_____

_____

_____

DAY 21

THE HEART OF JOY

Bring your awareness to a fault, grievance, or regret you have been carrying in your heart. Direct your breath inward, so it moves gently toward any sensations of tension or discomfort. Repeat the following: *May I be free. May I be kind to myself. May I move forward with simple joy.* With every inhalation and exhalation, connect with the capacity to open your heart to this moment. Finish the meditation by giving yourself a big hug, as if you are a cherished friend.

1. A fault, grievance, or regret that I would like to move forward through with simple joy is:

_____

_____

_____

_____

2. What would being kind to yourself and allowing yourself to move forward release for you?

_____

_____

_____

_____

3. A time I felt scared to confront a fault, grievance, or regret was:

_____

_____

_____

_____

MY INTENTION(S) FOR TODAY:

_____

_____

_____

_____

_____

_____

DAY 22

TUNE INTO COURAGE

Gently close your eyes and bring your awareness to your breath as you settle into an easy, natural rhythm of breathing. Inhale and exhale effortlessly through your nose. Notice where in your body you feel strong, courageous, and clear. Bring your awareness to that presence of inner strength and invite it to expand. Throughout your day, notice when you are centered in this gentle, quiet courage.

1. What are some feelings, thoughts, and sensations this meditation brought up for you?

_____

_____

_____

_____

2. When I think of being courageous, I:

_____

_____

_____

_____

3. I would like to be more courageous because:

_____

_____

_____

_____

MY INTENTION(S) FOR TODAY:

_____

_____

_____

_____

_____

_____

DAY 23

OPEN TO CURIOSITY

Stand with your feet hip-width apart and your eyes open. Slowly raise your arms so they are outstretched in front of you. How grounded, centered, and open do you feel in this moment? Are you at ease with being curious? Soften your fingers. Stretch your arms wider, as if you are holding more and more space between your hands. Experience this spaciousness and open yourself to curiosity.

1. An interaction or task I can bring my curiosity into today is:

_____

_____

_____

_____

2. What positive physical sensations accompany being open to curiosity?

_____

_____

_____

_____

3. A difficulty that I would like to bring curiosity to is:

_____

_____

_____

_____

MY INTENTION(S) FOR TODAY:

_____

_____

_____

_____

_____

_____

DAY 24

MAKE PEACE WITH YOUR INNER CRITIC

Find a comfortable position in which you feel supported. Breathing with your mouth closed, let yourself be enveloped by a warm current as you consciously invite in a "judgment" about yourself that you have struggled with. Meet your inner critic just as it is. Welcome its presence and let it rest in the space *around* your thoughts. With every exhalation, practice noticing your inner critic instead of reacting to it, and just let it float there without engaging. When you are done with this meditation, gently say goodbye to your inner critic.

1. Do you let your inner critic run wild, or do you take action to make peace with its presence?

_____

_____

_____

_____

2. How does it feel to consciously give a judgmental thought the gift of mental space?

_____

_____

_____

_____

3. Today I will make an effort to criticize myself and others less by:

_____

_____

_____

_____

MY INTENTION(S) FOR TODAY:

_____

_____

_____

_____

_____

_____

DAY 25

TRANSFORM NEGATIVE THOUGHTS

Settle into a comfortable position and soften any tension. Without trying to control your breath, gently inhale and exhale naturally. Imagine a space behind your mind's eye and think of one concern or negative perspective that currently troubles you. Envision the negative thought sinking into the vast spaciousness of your mind's eye and let it soften. Don't try to forcibly get rid of it. Just give your negative thought permission to dissolve.

1. Imagine a negative thought that has been with you for a while dissolving away. Can you describe what is happening? Are there any feelings or sensations associated with it?

_____

_____

_____

_____

2. Even though I feel _____, I totally and completely love myself for:

_____

_____

_____

_____

3. Bring a negative perspective to mind and try to see it visually, like on a screen. Now rotate it 180 degrees. How does it look now?

_____

_____

_____

_____

MY INTENTION(S) FOR TODAY:

_____

_____

_____

_____

_____

_____

DAY 26

PRACTICE RADICAL ACCEPTANCE

Invite a sense of well-being into this moment. Sitting quietly, repeat the following for several moments: *May I accept this life as it is. May I accept joy as it comes. May I accept where I am right now. May I accept the gift of today.* Next, think of one thing you are looking forward to. It can be small; what matters is that you attune to positivity. Give yourself permission to practice accepting joy today.

1. One difficult thing I need to begin to accept is:

_____

_____

_____

_____

2. Sometimes we are good at accepting pain but not joy. Are you able to accept joy in your life? How might you deepen your practice of accepting joy?

_____

_____

_____

_____

3. By accepting myself where I am right now, it might help me feel more:

_____

_____

_____

_____

MY INTENTION(S) FOR TODAY:

_____

_____

_____

_____

_____

_____

DAY 27

BE A MIRACLE SEEKER

Begin by placing your hands over your heart and turn your attention inward. Offer a quiet prayer of gratitude for your ability to notice everyday miracles. With your eyes softly closed, visualize your mind illuminated with light. Imagine a thread of light connecting your inner attention with your outer world. Instead of looking at what needs to be fixed or improved, challenge yourself to notice the miracles in every moment. Commit to being a miracle seeker.

1. One big miracle I would like to see in my life is:

_____

_____

_____

_____

2. Reflect on how you feel about everyday miracles. Do you notice them?

_____

_____

_____

_____

3. By looking for miraculous moments throughout my day, I feel more:

_____

_____

_____

_____

MY INTENTION(S) FOR TODAY:

_____

_____

_____

_____

_____

_____

DAY 28

TAP INTO SELF-LOVE

Find a comfortable, quiet place. Resting your hands wherever you wish, relax your fingers and loosen your jaw. As you soften your gaze or close your eyes, tap into the movement of your breath and imagine a quiet, powerful warmth deep within the center of your body. Visualize this warmth expanding as it fills your heart with luminosity. Tap into this momentum and notice the strong, nurturing presence of self-love.

1. One thing I love about myself is:

_____

_____

_____

_____

2. Think of a person in your life who reminds you to practice self-love. What are the qualities or characteristics about this person that inspire you?

_____

_____

_____

_____

3. I can love myself more today by:

_____

_____

_____

_____

MY INTENTION(S) FOR TODAY:

_____

_____

_____

_____

_____

_____

DAY 29

CONNECT WITH INNER CALM

Bring your awareness to your breath and settle into an easy, natural rhythm of breathing with your mouth closed. With each breath, connect with the present moment as you inhale calm and exhale chaos. With your mind's eye, imagine a day of calm awareness with minimal agitation and ease. Resting one hand on your heart and the other on your belly, invite the fullness of peace as you continue to breathe.

1. How does cultivating inner peace in difficult situations create a platform for empowered decision-making?

_____

_____

_____

_____

2. Imagine a future challenge or worry. How might it play out if you enter it with a connection to inner calm?

_____

_____

_____

_____

3. As you create space, distance, or time around a conflict, how does that conflict change for you?

_____

_____

_____

_____

MY INTENTION(S) FOR TODAY:

_____

_____

_____

_____

_____

_____

DAY 30

HEART ATTUNEMENT

Lie down with your eyes closed. Gently scan your body for sensations, beginning with your fingers and toes. As you inhale and exhale, move your attention slowly toward your heart. As you rest your awareness in the center of your heart, continue to breathe mindfully for several moments. With every inhalation, attune to the intelligence of your heart. Come into alignment with your natural, heartfelt presence, and imagine yourself radiating this heart-centered awareness.

1. Focusing your attention on your heart, write everything you notice about it.

_____

_____

_____

_____

2. How does your heart let you know when it needs to stay closed for safety or open for connection?

_____

_____

_____

_____

3. Imagine each beat of your heart is a thought or emotion. What are the next four beats of your heart?

_____

_____

_____

_____

MY INTENTION(S) FOR TODAY:

_____

_____

_____

_____

_____

_____

DAY 31

LIVE IN PURSUIT OF WONDER

In a seated position, rest your hands wherever you wish. Breathing through your nose with your mouth closed, tune into your inner space. Recall a simple memory of childlike wonder. Perhaps you feel wonder when you see a beautiful mountaintop view or a tender moment of kindness between two strangers. In moments of stress today, take time to recall this sensation of wonder and look for opportunities to be amazed by the quiet, wondrous joy of this life.

1. One memory of childlike wonder I recall is:

_____

_____

_____

_____

2. Now wonder feels like:

_____

_____

_____

_____

3. How often do you give yourself permission to experience this feeling? What might help you experience this feeling even more?

_____

_____

_____

_____

MY INTENTION(S) FOR TODAY:

_____

_____

_____

_____

_____

_____

DAY 32

VISUALIZE SERENDIPITY

Choose a comfortable place to sit or rest on your back. Imagine luminous threads of light connecting your inner space with your outer landscape. Let sounds come and go with ease. If there are no sounds, rest in this moment of silence. As you experience the expansive connectivity of your inner and outer worlds in this moment, take a moment to embrace the possibility of serendipity and happy chance. Invite mystical events to arise spontaneously and open yourself to unexpected joy.

1. What is an unexpected joy that you would like to experience today?

_____

_____

_____

_____

2. What are the qualities of unexpected joy?

_____

_____

_____

_____

3. What can you do physically to prepare for unexpected joy?

_____

_____

_____

_____

MY INTENTION(S) FOR TODAY:

_____

_____

_____

_____

_____

_____

DAY 33

FROM ANGER TO PASSION

Rest quietly and connect with the present moment. Anchor yourself in the center of your being as you reflect on the powerful sensation of anger in your body. Explore this emotional experience without self-judgment. Tune into the force behind the anger. As an experiment, ask yourself if your anger can be transformed *into passion* to become a bold, bright gift. Practice the art of approaching anger with mindful attention and radical hope.

1. After bringing to mind a situation in which you felt anger, surround the situation with the bright light of hope. How would you describe the anger to begin with, and what happens to the anger when you surround it with hope?

_____

_____

_____

_____

2. What would your anger tell you about what you need right now?

_____

_____

_____

_____

3. Imagine that radical hope or mindful attention is a healing salve you can rub on anger. What would that physically feel like in your body?

_____

_____

_____

_____

MY INTENTION(S) FOR TODAY:

_____

_____

_____

_____

_____

_____

DAY 34

THE WISDOM OF DOING LESS

Take a moment to rest quietly. Take in what is happening around you and connect with the stillness that exists beneath the busyness of the day ahead. Imagine what might happen if you harness the simple wisdom of doing less. Lean into the spaciousness of time and envision yourself replenishing your inner space. Instead of trying to accomplish as much as possible today, see how you can nurture your inner landscape. In doing so, you may notice more in your outer world.

1. Considering your to-do list for today and what is of utmost importance, what can you omit altogether or push off until tomorrow?

_____

_____

_____

_____

2. My top three priorities for today are:

_____

_____

_____

_____

3. How can I create more space to nurture my inner landscape?

_____

_____

_____

_____

MY INTENTION(S) FOR TODAY:

_____

_____

_____

_____

_____

_____

DAY 35

CONNECT WITH BOUNDLESS AWARENESS

Settle in for a gentle practice of nondirective attention and give your thoughts permission to arise, just as they are. Without trying to feel anything besides what you're feeling right now, breathe naturally as you open to the boundless awareness that is available to you in this moment. As your attention dissolves and emerges without effort, notice the subtle quality of remembrance. Turn toward presence again and again throughout your day and abide with the infinite potential of your attention.

1. How does it feel to allow your thoughts to arise without judgment?

_____

_____

_____

_____

2. Think of a moment later today or this week that you will bring boundless awareness to. What will you do differently, physically, in that moment?

_____

_____

_____

_____

3. What is the most comfortable position to be in to allow your attention to
dissolve and emerge without effort?

_____

_____

_____

_____

MY INTENTION(S) FOR TODAY:

_____

_____

_____

_____

_____

_____

DAY 36

RADIATE CONFIDENCE

Place your hands over your heart and gently turn your attention inward. With your eyes softly closed, visualize your heart illuminated with your favorite color. Tune into your ability to connect with the warm, subtle presence of your confidence, and thank it for its strength to transform. As you inhale and exhale with ease, envision this heartfelt luminosity expanding and growing stronger. Return to the present moment. Radiate with confidence whenever you wish.

1. Write a brief thank-you letter to your confidence for all that it does for you.

_____

_____

_____

_____

2. What are some moments today that you especially need your confidence to show up for you?

_____

_____

_____

_____

3. Make a plan for how you will invite and ensure your confidence is present when you need it most.

_____

_____

_____

_____

MY INTENTION(S) FOR TODAY:

_____

_____

_____

_____

_____

_____

DAY 37

SPACE FOR GRIEF

The greatest medicine for grief is kindness and compassion, and the decision to make space for overwhelming sensations can be a powerful way to practice self-care. Bring your awareness to the easy cadence of your breath and invite grief to be present. As you inhale and exhale, envelop your grief with a protective, warm spaciousness. As often as possible, let your grief breathe.

1. Write a letter to your grief.

_____

_____

_____

_____

2. If your grief had a physical location on your body, where would it be and why?

_____

_____

_____

_____

3. Describe one self-loving way to nurture yourself or others in times of grief.

_____

_____

_____

_____

MY INTENTION(S) FOR TODAY:

_____

_____

_____

_____

_____

_____

DAY 38

BUBBLE OF JOY

Imagine a large orb of soft, white light floating toward you. As it gets close enough for you to touch its outer perimeter, step inside of it. As you move into this bubble, notice what the light feels like—is it warm and soft? What sensations are you aware of? Remain in your bubble as long as you wish. Explore your invisible layer of joy.

1. Describe your bubble of joy.

_____

_____

_____

_____

2. What are the qualities of those who are welcome in your bubble of joy?

_____

_____

_____

_____

3. Where do you find aspects of your bubble of joy in your external world?

_____

_____

_____

_____

MY INTENTION(S) FOR TODAY:

_____

_____

_____

_____

_____

_____

DAY 39

HABITUAL OPTIMISM

As you come into harmony with the positivity available to you in each moment, it gets easier to notice specific elements of your day that inspire you to experience more presence. Rest in a comfortable space and take a moment to look around and notice three different things in your surroundings that you believe are beautiful. Do this multiple times throughout the day. By selecting three elements repeatedly, you are building a *pattern* of optimism. The more you practice this habit, the more it will become second nature.

1. List three events that you will encounter with glowing optimism today.

_____

_____

_____

_____

2. Complete this sentence: If someone _____ (an example of positivity and optimism), I will _____ (an action) to acknowledge it.

_____

_____

_____

_____

3. A jar full of optimism and positivity looks like:

_____

_____

_____

_____

MY INTENTION(S) FOR TODAY:

_____

_____

_____

_____

_____

_____

DAY 40

CELEBRATE TINY SUCCESS

Rest in a comfortable space and bring your attention to your breath. As you inhale and exhale naturally, invite your breath to be fluid. Bring one tiny success to mind. For example, sitting down to experience this meditation is worth celebrating! Instead of judging or rejecting a small victory for its size, let your success bring you joy. While resting in this moment of gratitude, practice mindful breathing. Welcome home to yourself.

1. Describe a tiny success you will experience today.

_____

_____

_____

_____

2. Write down as many tiny successes you could possibly experience in a day. Go!

_____

_____

_____

_____

3. Focus on one tiny success you have had and describe its physical effects on your body.

_____

_____

_____

_____

MY INTENTION(S) FOR TODAY:

_____

_____

_____

_____

_____

_____

DAY 41

EXPERIENCE INNER KNOWING

To develop confidence in your inner wisdom, cultivate the ability to connect with your felt sense of intuition. With practice, you can return to your inner knowing anytime you wish. Choose a comfortable position you can maintain for several moments. As you inhale and exhale gently with your eyes softly closed, tune into your internal landscape and the feeling of grounded knowing. Just for today, notice if you are willing to listen to what you know to be true.

1. A time when I knew something by my felt sense of intuition was:

_____

_____

_____

_____

2. What part of your body could serve as your personal barometer for intuition? How does it feel when it is active?

_____

_____

_____

_____

3. What superpower would you liken intuition to?

_____

_____

_____

_____

MY INTENTION(S) FOR TODAY:

_____

_____

_____

_____

_____

_____

DAY 42

PRESENCE WITH WHAT IS

Start by softening your gaze or closing your eyes. Bring your awareness to your breath and settle into an easy, natural rhythm of breathing. Resting with your mouth closed, inhale and exhale effortlessly through your nose. As you tune into your breath, connect with a vast inner awareness of the moment. Without exerting effort or trying to change anything, rest in who you are, right now. Notice how centered you feel when anchored to your own presence.

1. What are your primary feelings in this moment as you attune to the positive?

_____

_____

_____

_____

2. In this moment, I am aware of:

_____

_____

_____

_____

3. In the day ahead, when can you allow yourself to connect with your inner awareness of the moment?

_____

_____

_____

_____

MY INTENTION(S) FOR TODAY:

_____

_____

_____

_____

_____

_____

DAY 43

NOTICE YOUR RESILIENCE

Gently close your eyes and adjust your posture. Ground yourself in the present moment. Bring to mind a difficult or overwhelming emotion you have experienced recently. Resting with your mouth closed, inhale and exhale in an easy, natural rhythm. While holding your attention softly on the difficult emotion, tune into your inner resilience. Invite that resilience to envelope the difficult emotion you just recalled. Center yourself in the presence of your strength.

1. What are some feelings, thoughts, and sensations this meditation brought up for you?

_____

_____

_____

_____

2. What does your resilience look like?

_____

_____

_____

_____

3. One thing I can do today to feel stronger is:

_____

_____

_____

_____

MY INTENTION(S) FOR TODAY:

_____

_____

_____

_____

_____

_____

DAY 44

MINDFUL MEDIA EXPERIMENT

Television, social media, and various forms of digital information are known to cause anxiety, stress, and varying degrees of emotional unease. Since media is like food for your eyes, ears, and mind, take time to reflect on what you consume. Tune into your body and settle into the quality of your breath. Imagine how your mental clarity may respond to a choice to limit and be mindful of your media intake. For today, experiment by taking breaks from your screens and smartphone.

1. Take a few moments to reflect on the way you feel about digital media and how it impacts your well-being.

_____

_____

_____

_____

2. Instead of spending time on my smartphone or other devices, I can:

_____

_____

_____

_____

3. What might happen if you took an entire day off from social
media? A week?

_____

_____

_____

_____

MY INTENTION(S) FOR TODAY:

_____

_____

_____

_____

_____

_____

DAY 45

ENVISION YOUR TREE OF KNOWLEDGE

Gently close your eyes and imagine standing barefoot in a beautiful field. Feel the warmth of sunlight on your face and visualize a breeze moving across your skin. Notice a tree standing in a clearing, just behind your mind's eye. In the spaciousness all around it, there is a sense of familiarity, safety, and truth. Connect deeply with the energy here and return to this place whenever you wish.

1. Describe what your Tree of Knowledge looks like.

_____

_____

_____

_____

2. How often do you acknowledge your inner wisdom? When does it feel most accessible, and when does it not?

_____

_____

_____

_____

3. I know I am connected with my inner wisdom when:

_____

_____

_____

_____

MY INTENTION(S) FOR TODAY:

_____

_____

_____

_____

_____

_____

DAY 46

START THE DAY WITH AWARENESS

Use this simple practice to start your day with awareness. You can sit upright with your feet flat on the floor or lie down on your back. Take a few deep breaths and look around your environment to notice the present moment. Now tune into your body and let your breath soften into a natural flow that requires no effort. As you rest in mindful awareness, imagine taking this sensation of presence into your day.

1. Describe what you see in your immediate surroundings.

_____

_____

_____

_____

2. Describe what you hear right now in your environment.

_____

_____

_____

_____

3. By starting my day with awareness, I feel:

_____

_____

_____

_____

MY INTENTION(S) FOR TODAY:

_____

_____

_____

_____

_____

_____

DAY 47

THOUGHT CLOUDS

Start by softening your gaze or closing your eyes. Tune into your breath as it moves and settle into an easy, natural rhythm of breathing. Feel each breath moving in and out, as if it is a gentle breeze in the sky. Anytime a thought appears in your mind, treat it like a cloud that floats into view. Let these clouds move freely without trying to hold on to them or push them away. Notice how the breath can maintain its effortless movement, even as these thought clouds come and go.

1. Write the weather report for today, with the conditions representing your thoughts.

_____

_____

_____

_____

2. I know my brain is tired and I need a break when:

_____

_____

_____

_____

3. Describe your favorite weather and your favorite season.

_____

_____

_____

_____

MY INTENTION(S) FOR TODAY:

_____

_____

_____

_____

_____

_____

DAY 48

CENTERED IN SPACE

This exercise can be done seated or standing up. Begin by resting your arms comfortably at your sides. Connect with the pull of gravity beneath you and take this moment to center yourself in time and space before beginning your day. When you feel anchored within, slowly raise your arms in front of you. Then slowly lower them. Repeat this movement three to five times. Notice how you can feel centered even when there is movement all around you.

1. What are some moments in your upcoming day that you would like to feel centered and grounded?

_____

_____

_____

_____

2. What are some small or inconspicuous motions you can make to center yourself during your day?

_____

_____

_____

_____

3. I feel most grounded when:

_____

_____

_____

_____

MY INTENTION(S) FOR TODAY:

_____

_____

_____

_____

_____

_____

DAY 49

NOURISHING PRESENCE

Settle in for a gentle practice of nondirective awareness and tune into your innermost feelings about your relationship with food. Without trying to change anything about how you feel right now, breathe naturally as you open to the subtle quality of presence you are able to bring to each meal. As your attention emerges and dissolves without effort, imagine this quality of presence expanding from within. Turn toward what nourishes you; abide with sensations of healing.

1. I feel nourished by:

_____

_____

_____

_____

2. Describe a relationship that nourishes you.

_____

_____

_____

_____

3. Is it possible to have too much of a good thing—to be overly nourished? Why or why not?

_____

_____

_____

_____

MY INTENTION(S) FOR TODAY:

_____

_____

_____

_____

_____

_____

DAY 50

ALTERNATE NOSTRIL BREATHING

Choose a quiet setting and sit in a relaxed, seated position with your eyes open or closed. Use your right thumb to close your right nostril, and inhale slowly through your left nostril. Pause, then close your left nostril with your right ring and/or pinkie finger, and exhale slowly through your right nostril. Pause, then inhale through your right nostril. Continue to switch back and forth while using your thumb and ring/pinkie fingers. Notice how you feel after several breaths.

1. What are some thoughts, feelings, and sensations that came up for you during this exercise?

_____

_____

_____

_____

2. What are slight changes you can make to one regular activity in your day (e.g., toothbrushing, eating, etc.) to be more present?

_____

_____

_____

_____

3. What benefits do your routines provide you with?

_____

_____

_____

_____

MY INTENTION(S) FOR TODAY:

_____

_____

_____

_____

_____

_____

DAY 51

INHALE GRATITUDE

With your eyes softly closed, breathe in and out gently. Bring to mind one thing in your life that you feel grateful for. With every inhalation and every exhalation, think to yourself, "I am grateful for _____." Tune into your ability to connect with the warm, subtle presence of gratitude and thank it for its strength. Cherish this feeling as you return to the present moment and try to carry it with you throughout your day.

1. How can you more fully inhale gratitude, in the moment, during your experiences?

_____

_____

_____

_____

2. The thing I feel the most gratitude for right now is:

_____

_____

_____

_____

3. If gratitude had a sound, what would it be?

_____

_____

_____

_____

MY INTENTION(S) FOR TODAY:

_____

_____

_____

_____

_____

_____

DAY 52

NOTICE THE GOOD STUFF

Start by softening your gaze and bringing awareness to your breath as you settle into an easy, natural rhythm of breathing. Inhale and exhale effortlessly through your nose. As you tune into your breath, connect with what is truly good in your life, right now. With every inhalation and exhalation, feel this goodness expand. Now, bring your awareness back to the present moment. Commit to noticing what is good.

1. The truly good things in my life that I sometimes overlook are:

_____

_____

_____

_____

2. Think of some of the challenges you face in life. What good can you identify in these challenges?

_____

_____

_____

_____

3. I can remind myself to notice the good things in my life by:

_____

_____

_____

_____

MY INTENTION(S) FOR TODAY:

_____

_____

_____

_____

_____

_____

DAY 53

TAKING BREAKS

Choose a comfortable position you can maintain for several moments. Bring your attention to the day ahead and mentally travel into your future. In your mind's eye, visualize your schedule for the day. Notice where you have (and have not) planned to take any breaks between appointments, responsibilities, or time with others. How often do you give yourself time to rest? Make a conscious choice to find time today to recharge—even five minutes can have a positive impact.

1. What would you pack in your virtual "break pack"? Describe what you need to optimize your break (mindful breathing, a cup of tea, stretching, etc.).

_____

_____

_____

_____

2. Write down a plan for taking breaks between meetings or tasks.

_____

_____

_____

_____

3. By taking breaks and practicing self-care, I will feel more:

_____

_____

_____

_____

MY INTENTION(S) FOR TODAY:

_____

_____

_____

_____

_____

_____

DAY 54

ENCOURAGE OTHERS

With your eyes open or closed, center yourself in your breath and imagine a warm sensation of generosity expanding from your heart. With every inhalation, tune into a feeling of joy, and with every exhalation, imagine yourself sharing this joy and offering encouragement to others in your life. Inhale and exhale gently; let yourself be enveloped by a current of empathetic connectivity. Open yourself up to supporting others with kind words and thoughtful attention.

1. Write down some encouraging things you can say to people as you move through your day.

_____

_____

_____

_____

2. What do you notice about yourself when you say something encouraging to others?

_____

_____

_____

_____

3. I would like to try encouraging others more often because:

_____

_____

_____

_____

MY INTENTION(S) FOR TODAY:

_____

_____

_____

_____

_____

_____

DAY 55

TRANSFORM TENSION

Find a quiet place to sit and settle into a comfortable position of ease. Begin by taking three calming breaths, counting to six as you exhale. Shrug your shoulders tight toward your ears, and then let your shoulders relax. Inhale again slowly as you repeat the same three calming breaths and soften any tension. Whenever possible, let there be space in your body for effortless, gentle flow.

1. If you felt more relaxed today, how might that impact your flow?

_____

_____

_____

_____

2. What does tension feel like in your body?

_____

_____

_____

_____

3. I can self-soothe and transform tension today by:

_____

_____

_____

_____

MY INTENTION(S) FOR TODAY:

_____

_____

_____

_____

_____

_____

DAY 56

MAKE PEACE WITH IMPERMANENCE

Rest your palms wherever you wish and begin to inhale and exhale gently. Notice your deep, abiding strength as you center yourself in your breath. Invite a sense of peace into this moment. Repeat the following quietly for several moments: *May I be at peace with this life. May I be at ease with impermanence. May I face change with courage.* Bring your awareness back to this peace whenever you wish.

1. Bring to mind an anticipated change or transition, however big or small, and describe the positive benefits of this change.

_____

_____

_____

_____

2. Dear courage, you can show up for me today by:

_____

_____

_____

_____

3. What I love most about my life right now is:

_____

_____

_____

_____

MY INTENTION(S) FOR TODAY:

_____

_____

_____

_____

_____

_____

DAY 57

MORNING THOUGHTS

Without trying to control your breath, gently inhale and exhale naturally. For a few moments, notice whatever thoughts arise, paying particular attention to the sensation of calm that rests in the space *between* your thoughts. As you begin your day, tune into this pattern of ebb and flow and bring a sense of presence to your morning. Offer a quiet prayer of gratitude for your ability to attune to the wisdom of your breath and solve problems with joy.

1. Take a moment to tune into the weather outside this morning. What do you like about it?

_____

_____

_____

_____

2. One thing I am grateful for in this moment is:

_____

_____

_____

_____

3. The part of me that feels most calm right now is _____. I know this because:

_____

_____

_____

_____

MY INTENTION(S) FOR TODAY:

_____

_____

_____

_____

_____

_____

DAY 58

GRATITUDE FOR YOUR BODY

Take a few breaths and settle into the present moment as you tune into your body. Notice sensations of temperature, pressure, gravity, and lightness. Bring your awareness to various parts of your body and thank them for supporting you from one day to the next. As your attention moves from one area to another, express gratitude for each and every part of you. Place your hands over your heart and tell your body *thank you*.

1. What is one part of your body that works tirelessly and is especially deserving of your appreciation? Describe something amazing that this body part does.

_____

_____

_____

_____

2. I can show gratitude for my body by:

_____

_____

_____

_____

3. Write a thank-you letter to your body for all that it does for you.

_____

_____

_____

_____

MY INTENTION(S) FOR TODAY:

_____

_____

_____

_____

_____

_____

DAY 59

BEFRIENDING YOURSELF

Begin by softening your gaze or closing your eyes. Bring your awareness to your breath and settle into an easy, natural rhythm of breathing. Take this time to reflect on how you can be a better friend to *yourself*. With each breath, visualize self-judgment transforming into self-love. With your mind's eye, imagine a day of befriending your innermost feelings. As you rest one hand on your heart, invite gentle warmth into this moment.

1. Describe the ways your ideal best friend would show up for you.

_____

_____

_____

_____

2. One thing I can do today to show myself self-love is:

_____

_____

_____

_____

3. As if you are your own best friend, write an encouraging and compassionate note to yourself to read later in the day or week.

_____

_____

_____

_____

MY INTENTION(S) FOR TODAY:

_____

_____

_____

_____

_____

_____

DAY 60

THE INNER JOY ATTUNEMENT

This exercise is done lying down with your eyes closed. Breathing naturally, bring to mind someone or something you care for deeply. As you inhale and exhale, tune into what is joyful about this person, place, thing, or experience. Invite this joy to expand throughout your mind, heart, and breath. Notice your body begin to relax and allow yourself to ease into this sensation. Continue to breathe mindfully for several moments.

1. The joy that _____ (person/thing) brings me feels like:

_____

_____

_____

_____

2. I care for _____ (person/thing) deeply because:

_____

_____

_____

_____

3. Describe one joy you're looking forward to experiencing later today or this week.

_____

_____

_____

_____

MY INTENTION(S) FOR TODAY:

_____

_____

_____

_____

_____

_____

DAY 61

EMBRACE UNCERTAINTY

Sit comfortably and rest your hands wherever you wish. Breathing through your nose with your mouth closed, tune into your internal landscape. Feel the natural rhythm of your inner world as you breathe and know that you can count on this reliable source of steadiness whenever uncertainty arises. The practice of embracing uncertainty is supported by the stability of this inhale and exhale. A sense of flow can deepen over time. Turn your attention to this centered ease.

1. Imagine giving your uncertainty a big hug. What happens when you stop resisting uncertainty?

_____

_____

_____

_____

2. I can cope with uncertainty better by:

_____

_____

_____

_____

3. It is courageous to allow space for uncertainty. Write a note of encouragement to yourself to read whenever uncertainty causes you distress.

_____

_____

_____

_____

MY INTENTION(S) FOR TODAY:

_____

_____

_____

_____

_____

_____

DAY 62

THE GIFT OF SPONTANEOUS INSPIRATION

Begin by imagining a space behind your mind's eye. As this space expands, give yourself permission to receive the gift of spontaneous inspiration today. Rest in the awareness that creativity is grounded in gentle presence and you can tap into it anytime. Notice if colors, ideas, or thoughts come to mind. As often as possible, let there be space for spontaneous inspiration. Take time to appreciate new ideas that come and go with ease.

1. I feel spontaneous inspiration when:

_____

_____

_____

_____

2. I can support my creativity today by:

_____

_____

_____

_____

3. Writing from a place of deep appreciation for your creativity, write a free flow poem. Once your pen touches the paper, don't stop writing until you feel complete.

_____

_____

_____

_____

MY INTENTION(S) FOR TODAY:

_____

_____

_____

_____

_____

_____

DAY 63

PAUSE WORRY

Bring your awareness to a worry you have been carrying. Direct your breath inward so it moves gently toward any sensations of tension or discomfort. In your mind's eye, imagine that you can see an oversized pause button and mentally push it. By consciously interrupting the cycle of repetitive worrying, you create space for your mind to rest. With every inhalation and exhalation, connect with your capacity to resolve difficulties that cause distress.

1. What might happen if you take a vacation from worrying today?

_____

_____

_____

_____

2. Without dismissing your worry, identify aspects of your worry that you can learn from.

_____

_____

_____

_____

3. How can you manage your concerns or worries in a way that is positive?

_____

_____

_____

_____

MY INTENTION(S) FOR TODAY:

_____

_____

_____

_____

_____

_____

DAY 64

YOUR AUTHENTIC SELF

Rest quietly and connect with the present moment to consider how authentic you are with others. Reflect without self-judgment. Bring an upcoming conversation to your mind's eye and experiment with the practice of approaching it with genuine authenticity. If you feel anxious about expressing yourself, choose a mantra for inner support. Select a word to use as an anchor in moments of doubt or fear and repeat it silently: truth, compassion, courage, or hope.

1. Write a certificate of authenticity for yourself, listing qualities others admire about you.

_____

_____

_____

_____

2. People are fortunate to have me in their lives because:

_____

_____

_____

_____

3. I can create space for my true self to shine today by prioritizing:

_____

_____

_____

_____

MY INTENTION(S) FOR TODAY:

_____

_____

_____

_____

_____

_____

DAY 65

MIND OF SKY

Settle in for a gentle practice of nondirective attention. Rest in the simple presence of this moment and abide with what is. Envision your mind as an open, cloudless sky, and whenever you notice a thought, feeling, or physical sensation, let it arise. Give your thoughts permission to come and go as if they are clouds moving across the vast blue expanse of your inner landscape. Practice awakening to the subtle qualities of your attention.

1. What did you enjoy about this meditation practice?

_____

_____

_____

_____

2. Thoughts are like clouds in a sky because:

_____

_____

_____

_____

3. When I pay attention to the present moment, I feel:

_____

_____

_____

_____

MY INTENTION(S) FOR TODAY:

_____

_____

_____

_____

_____

_____

DAY 66

EMBODY FRIENDLINESS

Place your hands over your heart and turn your attention inward. With your eyes softly closed, visualize your heart illuminated with warmth. Thank it for its strength to embody a friendly, generous presence. As you inhale and exhale with ease, envision this warmth expanding. Notice the gentle presence of friendliness and joy. Return to the present moment and carry this sensation into your day. Share presence, experience connection, and rest in heartfelt awareness.

1. My heart is a muscle. Three things I can do today to exercise it are:

_____

_____

_____

_____

2. I am grateful for my heart because it enables me to:

_____

_____

_____

_____

3. Today I will share my heartfelt awareness with myself and others by:

_____

_____

_____

_____

MY INTENTION(S) FOR TODAY:

_____

_____

_____

_____

_____

_____

MOUNTAIN MEDITATION

Sitting comfortably, visualize an image of a mountain in your mind's eye. Allow the sturdy and reliable weight of this mountain to sink into your being. Let your body and the mountain become one. Grounded and centered in stillness, your head becomes the peak, and your body is the deep, solid stone that remains grounded in any kind of weather. Feeling secure and complete, celebrate your strength.

1. Give your inner mountain a secret name and explain what it means.

_____

_____

_____

_____

2. What are positive thoughts you can count on as you move through your day?

_____

_____

_____

_____

3. Describe yourself as a mountain of grounded and centered stillness.

_____

_____

_____

_____

MY INTENTION(S) FOR TODAY:

_____

_____

_____

_____

_____

_____

DAY 68

EMBRACE THE VULNERABILITY OF JOY

Researcher and author Brené Brown has said that joy is the most vulnerable emotion we ever feel. Focus your efforts today on embracing the vulnerability of joy. Notice whether you tend to push joy away or allow yourself to receive this radically tender feeling. Take a few moments to imagine a space behind your mind's eye, and as this space expands, give yourself permission to fill it with joy. Rest in this awareness and as often as possible, protect your right to joy.

1. Tune into the emotional feeling of joy and describe it.

_____

_____

_____

_____

2. Imagine joy is a hot air balloon carrying you up into the sky. What do you see as you rise?

_____

_____

3. Bring to mind a recent experience of joy and describe its physical effect on you.

_____

_____

_____

_____

MY INTENTION(S) FOR TODAY:

_____

_____

_____

_____

_____

_____

DAY 69

FOLLOW A DREAM

Begin by closing your eyes and relaxing your whole body. Breathing naturally, connect with your inner landscape and loosen the muscles around your face, especially the jaw. Close your eyes and think of a dream or goal that is important to you. Mentally think of one step you can take today to follow this dream. Envision yourself enveloped by courage and strength. Give yourself permission to move forward with powerful optimism.

1. How does it feel to dream? Exciting? Frightening? Why do you think that is?

_____

_____

_____

_____

2. Someone I can talk to about my dream is _____ because:

_____

_____

_____

_____

3. The action I need to take to help me make my dream come true is:

_____

_____

_____

_____

MY INTENTION(S) FOR TODAY:

_____

_____

_____

_____

_____

_____

DAY 70

EMPOWER YOUR DESIRE FOR MORE

Soften your gaze or close your eyes as you bring your awareness to your breath and settle into an easy, natural rhythm of breathing. Resting with your mouth closed, inhale and exhale effortlessly. As you tune into your breath, connect with what you truly desire more of in your life. Perhaps it is a new job or a loving relationship. Whatever it may be, give yourself permission to experience an important and meaningful longing.

1. Reflect on how it feels to give yourself permission to experience desire.

_____

_____

_____

_____

2. Something I desire more of in life is:

_____

_____

_____

_____

3. Write a letter to yourself that gives you permission to have what you truly desire.

_____

_____

_____

_____

MY INTENTION(S) FOR TODAY:

_____

_____

_____

_____

_____

_____

DAY 71

MANAGING TIME

Bring your attention to the day ahead and mentally travel into your future. In your mind's eye, visualize your schedule. Do you find that you tend to need more time than you actually give yourself for appointments and responsibilities, or travel between them? How might you give yourself the gift of more generously managing your time, so your schedule isn't rushed? Make a conscious choice to tune into how much time you need from one moment to the next.

1. Something I am looking forward to today is:

_____

_____

_____

_____

2. Managing my time carefully can help me to:

_____

_____

_____

_____

3. One thing I can do to move confidently from one task to the
next today is:

_____

_____

_____

_____

MY INTENTION(S) FOR TODAY:

_____

_____

_____

_____

_____

_____

DAY 72

SLOW DOWN TO GO FAST

Often the act of slowing down and being mindful can make your workflow more efficient and reduce the likelihood of making a mistake. Settle into a comfortable position of ease. Begin by taking three calming breaths, and count to six as you exhale. Shrug your shoulders tight toward your ears, and then let your shoulders relax. Whenever possible throughout your day, give yourself the gift of mindfulness and remind yourself that you can slow down to go fast.

1. What are three things you can do more slowly today?

_____

_____

_____

_____

2. What happens in your body when you slow down?

_____

_____

_____

_____

3. How can you give yourself a gentle reminder to slow down?

_____

_____

_____

_____

MY INTENTION(S) FOR TODAY:

_____

_____

_____

_____

_____

_____

DAY 73

INNER HEALING VISUALIZATION

Imagine a space behind your mind's eye. As this space expands, fill it with a soft, warm light. Rest in this awareness and notice any color that may arise. Envision this light as a healing energy illuminating you from within so that you are both emanating and absorbing a luminosity that is independent of your outer environment. Imagine a thread of light connecting your mind with your heart and notice sensations of calm spreading throughout your body.

1. Take a moment to reflect on how this practice felt.

_____

_____

_____

_____

2. Design and describe a forcefield between you and your outer environment that is capable of transforming external stimuli before they come in contact with you. The sound of a horn honking becomes _____. The rain becomes _____.

_____

_____

_____

_____

3. What are supportive and nurturing elements from your external world that you can say thank you to?

_____

_____

_____

_____

MY INTENTION(S) FOR TODAY:

_____

_____

_____

_____

_____

_____

DAY 74

WAVES OF HOPE

Stand in a comfortable position and visualize gentle waves. Imagine one of them is rolling gently toward you. As if you are surrounded by an ocean of hope, notice the water's calm strength. Breathing with your mouth closed, let yourself be enveloped by a warm flow that holds you with quiet ease. Bring your awareness back to the moment and notice any sensations. Remember this wave of hope and comfort whenever you feel despair or sadness.

1. What happens if you imagine positive outcomes before potential obstacles?

_____

_____

_____

_____

2. One part of my day I want to infuse with hope is:

_____

_____

_____

_____

3. If you felt more hope throughout your day, how would your day be different?

_____

_____

_____

_____

MY INTENTION(S) FOR TODAY:

_____

_____

_____

_____

_____

_____

_____

DAY 75

COHERENT BREATHING FOR STRESS

This simple practice is known to have metabolic and cognitively restorative benefits. Choose a comfortable position, either sitting or lying down, and soften any tension. Connect with your breath. With your mouth closed, gently inhale through your nose as you count to six. Again with your mouth closed, gently exhale through your nose as you count to six. Repeat this breathing technique for five minutes. Know that you can return to this practice at any time throughout your day to ground yourself in moments of stress.

1. Three things I have done well this week are (e.g., brushing my teeth, managing my schedule, etc.):

_____

_____

_____

_____

2. Challenges I will allow to exist alongside my joy and happiness are:

_____

_____

_____

_____

3. One thing I love about myself is:

_____

_____

_____

_____

MY INTENTION(S) FOR TODAY:

_____

_____

_____

_____

_____

_____

DAY 76

ABIDING PRACTICE: NOTHING TO FIX TODAY

Fixing problems or changing circumstances can become a compulsive habit that prevents us from being present in the moment. Sometimes it is healthy to take a break from fixing and just accept what is. Place your hands over your heart and turn your attention inward. Offer a quiet prayer of gratitude for what you have. Appreciate this life just as it is. Thank your mind for its ability to solve difficult problems, and then tell it that *there is nothing to fix*. Today, give your brilliant mind a rest.

1. At this very moment I am grateful for:

_____

_____

_____

_____

2. If I take a break from fixing today, I might have more time to:

_____

_____

_____

_____

3. I deserve to give my mind a rest because:

_____

_____

_____

_____

MY INTENTION(S) FOR TODAY:

_____

_____

_____

_____

_____

_____

DAY 77

THE PRACTICE OF *BOTH, AND*

Wisdom becomes available when you realize you are allowed to experience joy and pain *at the same time*; you do not have to choose one or the other. Rest or close your eyes and imagine yourself holding both of these feelings deep inside, in the same inner space. What does it feel like to give yourself permission to hold all of yourself with resolute tenderness, without choosing one feeling over another? It is unnecessary to deny yourself joy because you feel pain. There is no need to abandon pain because you believe that joy is better. Instead of choosing one emotion, try centering yourself in the wisdom of wholeness, and trust there is a safe space in the sanctuary of your being— for all emotion to breathe with ease. This is the practice of *Both, And*.

1. I know I am experiencing joy when I feel/sense/think:

_____

_____

_____

_____

2. When I think of feeling both joy and pain at the same time, it feels:

_____

_____

_____

_____

3. An upcoming challenge today that may provide me with an opportunity
to practice Both, And is:

_____

_____

_____

_____

MY INTENTION(S) FOR TODAY:

_____

_____

_____

_____

_____

_____

DAY 78

TUNE INTO GRACE

By offering yourself grace, you are giving yourself the gift of kindness and mercy. Soften your gaze and rest your eyes on a point in your surroundings. Inhale slowly and begin to hum quietly on your exhale. As you feel the vibration of the hum moving throughout your body, imagine it carries a quality of grace or goodwill. Take the sound and presence of grace into your day and tune into it as needed.

1. I can show myself goodwill today by:

_____

_____

_____

_____

2. What can you show yourself grace for today?

_____

_____

_____

_____

3. My smile has the power to:

_____

_____

_____

_____

MY INTENTION(S) FOR TODAY:

_____

_____

_____

_____

_____

_____

DAY 79

I AM ALWAYS WORTHY

Connect with a sense of stillness in this moment. Resting your palms wherever you wish, begin to inhale and exhale gently. Notice yourself slow down and center yourself in your breath. Repeat the following mantra quietly: *I am worthy right now. I am worthy as I am. I have always been worthy. I will always be worthy.* Bring your awareness back to the power of your worthiness whenever you wish.

1. Today I will show up with my best self by:

_____

_____

_____

_____

2. Feeling worthy and valued feels like:

_____

_____

_____

_____

3. Something I can do to remind myself that I have always been worthy is:

_____

_____

_____

_____

MY INTENTION(S) FOR TODAY:

_____

_____

_____

_____

_____

_____

"FOREVER IS COMPOSED OF NOWS."

—*Emily Dickinson*

PARTING WORDS

Heartfelt mindfulness is the practice of acknowledging that we are worthy of what we long to recover of ourselves, worthy of what we love about each other, and worthy of a shared experience in which each of us plays a vital, sacred part. The awareness we bring to our mornings becomes the fabric of our waking days, and by practicing meditation, we bring more clarity and perspective to this human experience while encouraging others to do the same.

To be present with this life is an act of radical courage and dignity. By making a choice to commit to a morning meditation routine, you have expanded conscious awareness, nourished vast neural networks, and successfully built a soothing habit of simple (yet profound) self-care. You are more equipped to accept anguish or discomfort with grace. As your experience of a felt sense of joy evolves, your mindfulness journey can be a nourishing resource—and a reminder of your natural instinct to heal from within. I honor the time you've set aside for yourself, and I celebrate the work you've done to offer yourself the enduring gift of presence. Remember, even five minutes a day is sufficient to create sustainable, positive change in your neurochemistry. I hope the sense of ease and well-being you have experienced will continue to tether you to a wellspring of hope, quiet warmth, and luminous inspiration. As you reflect on the journey you've taken with this journal, I encourage you to carry your most favorite meditations forward. As often as possible, connect with a soft-hearted commitment to explore the myriad of ways you might bring these practices into your life.

This book and these practices are here for you whenever you need them. For ongoing support or further learning, I encourage you to explore wisdom traditions that speak to you personally and experiment with mindfulness practices you feel called to try. If you prefer to practice with others, you may want to find a meditation group or sangha (a

Buddhist term for spiritual community) in order to share your spiritual journey with others. On the other hand, if you prefer to practice in solitude, I suggest you choose one to three favorite meditation techniques and challenge yourself to meet your innermost self more deeply by practicing one of these meditations at the same time every morning, for a minimum of 30 days in a row. By doing so, you will discover how meditation can be an anchor, an ally, and a guide home to yourself, regardless of what is happening in your environment or the greater world.

You may feel confused or insecure about whether you are doing it "correctly," which is a natural part of meditation. Even the most advanced meditation practitioners in the world struggle at times, because the journey of presence is changeable; all of us are learning. All of us are discovering new inner gifts on our way home to ourselves. Practice, not perfection, is a path of enduring self-love. Your breath is an anchor you can return to again and again, and your inner wisdom is always accessible. To know oneself intimately is the soul's greatest longing, and there is power in your capacity to hold yourself with tender, abiding warmth.

I wish you the very best on this journey of remembrance; my heart travels with you.

RESOURCES

BOOKS

Aware: The Science and Practice of Presence by Daniel J. Siegel, MD

The Healing Power of the Breath: Simple Techniques to Reduce Stress and Anxiety, Enhance Concentration, and Balance Your Emotions by Richard P. Brown, MD and Patricia L. Gerberg, MD

The CBT Deck: 101 Practices to Improve Thoughts, Be in the Moment & Take Action in Your Life by Seth J. Gillihan, PhD

Atomic Habits: An Easy & Proven Way to Build Good Habits & Break New Ones by James Clear

10% Happier by Sam Harris

ONLINE

Insight Timer (InsightTimer.com)
App and online community for meditation.

Headspace (Headspace.com)
App for mindfulness and meditation.

TaraBrach.com
Website of psychologist and meditation teacher Tara Brach, with several meditations and other resources.

Recovery Dharma (RecoveryDharma.com)
Buddhist-based program and fellowship for recovery from addiction.

REFERENCES

Brach, Tara. "Feeling Overwhelmed? Remember RAIN." Mindful. January 13, 2016. Accessed December, 2020. https://www.mindful.org/tara-brach-rain-mindfulness-practice/.

Brown, Brené. *Dare to Lead: Brave Work. Tough Conversations*. Whole Hearts. New York: Random House, 2018.

Frangello, Gina. "Both/And: A Conversation with Emily Rapp Black." Los Angeles Review of Books. March 17, 2021. https://lareviewofbooks.org/article/both-and-a-conversation-with-emily-rapp-black/.

ABOUT THE AUTHOR

WORTHY STOKES is a bestselling author and the founder of The HeartMind® Process. Her warm, personable teaching style reflects an embodied spiritual perspective that is grounded in years of advanced contemplative practice, and her guided HeartMind® meditations have touched thousands across the world. Learn more about her at WorthyStokes.com.

CPSIA information can be obtained
at www.ICGtesting.com
Printed in the USA
JSHW042100170721
16980JS00001B/2